INCREDIBLE INSECTS

written by Lori C. Froeb
reviewed by Louis N. Sorkin, B.C.E.

Reader's Digest Children's Books®

Pleasantville, New York • Montréal, Québec • Bath, United Kingdom

What Is an Insect?

You see them all around you—in the trees, underground, in the water, even in your house! They are insects, and we share the world with 30 million of them! But what are insects?

All insects have several things in common. They all belong to a group of animals called **arthropods**. Instead of bones like you have, they have a tough outer shell called an **exoskeleton**. The exoskeleton is very light and strong and protects the insect's insides.

Every insect's body is divided into three parts: the head, thorax, and abdomen.

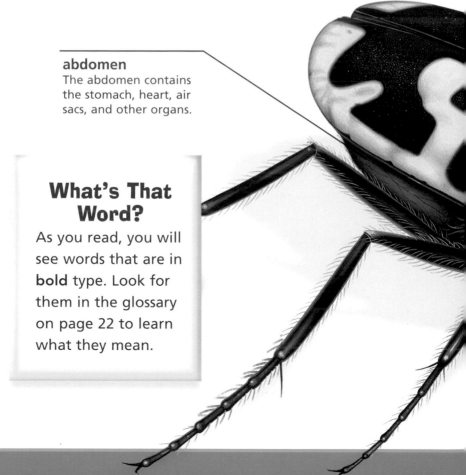

abdomen
The abdomen contains the stomach, heart, air sacs, and other organs.

What's That Word?

As you read, you will see words that are in **bold** type. Look for them in the glossary on page 22 to learn what they mean.

The head has the eyes, antennae, mouthparts, and brain. The head is attached to the thorax. The insect's wings and six legs are attached to the thorax. The abdomen holds all the guts.

Now that you know the basics, let's get to know some of our creeping, crawling neighbors better!

Did You Know?
Cockroaches were among the very first land insects. Scientists have found cockroach fossils that are up to 300 million years old!

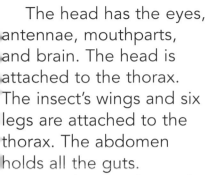

thorax
The legs and wings are attached to the thorax.

head
The head is one of the strongest body parts—good protection for the brain.

Tiger Beetle

Sense-sational

Insects have the same senses as you do—smell, touch, sight, taste, and hearing. But what parts do they have for using their senses? Do insects have ears? Tongues?

The antennae are two of the most important parts of an insect's body. Antennae are used to smell, touch, and hear. When it comes to seeing, insects have two eyes, like you. But each eye is made up of many little lenses. This lets the insect see all around its body—even the smallest movement.

Insects taste their food before eating using sense organs near the mouth called **palps**. Some insects, like butterflies and flies, can taste through their feet—letting them know when something they land on is good to eat. Instead of ears, many insects use their antennae and fine body hairs to hear.

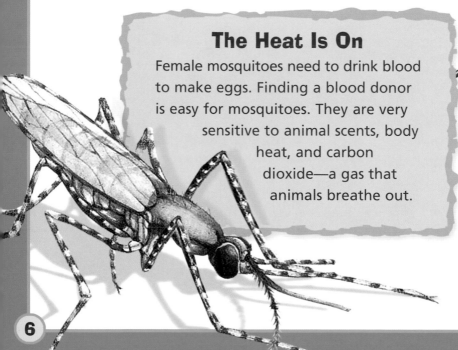

The Heat Is On

Female mosquitoes need to drink blood to make eggs. Finding a blood donor is easy for mosquitoes. They are very sensitive to animal scents, body heat, and carbon dioxide—a gas that animals breathe out.

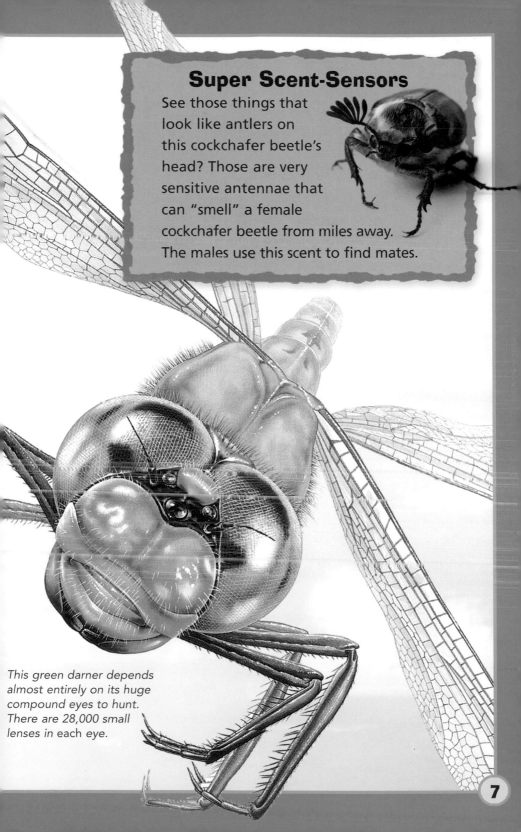

Super Scent-Sensors

See those things that look like antlers on this cockchafer beetle's head? Those are very sensitive antennae that can "smell" a female cockchafer beetle from miles away. The males use this scent to find mates.

This green darner depends almost entirely on its huge compound eyes to hunt. There are 28,000 small lenses in each eye.

Oh, Baby!

When it comes to reproducing, insects are pros! Every insect begins life as an egg. Most eggs are laid near plenty of food so that the young have lots to eat when they are born. Insect babies grow FAST, but their exoskeletons can't. They must shed, or molt, their old exoskeletons to grow. Every time they molt, they get bigger and change shape. Once they are adults, they stop molting. This process is called **metamorphosis**.

Some insects look a little like their parents when they are born. They are called nymphs. They go through a simple metamorphosis to grow— changing gradually until they become adults. Some nymphs—like aphids and bedbugs—look just like their parents. Others look very different—and even live in different environments. For example, dragonfly nymphs (called naiads) live underwater. They crawl onto land for their last molt and, after drying, fly away!

Did You Know?

Ladybugs lay their eggs on leaves where aphids feed. As soon as a larva hatches, it quickly starts gobbling all the aphids in sight. It will eat about 400 of them before turning into an adult.

Roly-poly Nursery

Dung beetles lay their eggs in a very strange place—on animal poop! After carefully rolling dung into a ball, the female lays one egg inside. Eventually, the larva will hatch inside its nursery and enjoy its first meal—dung.

Painted grasshoppers use sound to attract females. They rub pegs on their hind legs against ridges on their wings to make a loud rasping noise. The females hear the males' songs and choose a mate.

Presto, Change-o!

Some insect babies look absolutely nothing like their parents. These insects don't change shape gradually. They do it all at once—in a process called complete metamorphosis. When they hatch, they are called larvae. They have soft bodies, no wings, and sometimes have no legs, either! Butterfly and moth larvae are usually called caterpillars. Most fly larvae are called maggots, and most beetle larvae are called grubs.

A larva eats nonstop, and molts several times. Once it is full-sized, it stops eating and moving. This means it's ready to pupate—or finally change into an adult. The larva may become a **pupa** or spin a **cocoon**. During this stage, its body forms all the adult features. When it is finished, it has wings and the ability to reproduce. The new butterfly, beetle, or fly will often eat different foods and live in a different habitat than it did when it was a larva. It's a major change of life!

Did You Know?

Each silkworm cocoon is made of a single thread of silk that can be up to 3,000 feet long (that's more than half a mile)! Silk makers boil silkworm cocoons to harvest their silk thread and make it into cloth.

eggs

caterpillar

This picture shows all the life stages of the Indian moon moth—from egg to new moth. After it leaves the cocoon, the moth must let its new wings stretch and harden before flying for the first time.

cocoon

Indian moon moth

Eaten Alive!

A female wasp laid eggs inside this hornworm caterpillar. The larvae hatched and hungrily ate the caterpillar from the inside out. Then they burst through its skin and turned into the white pupae you see here.

What's for Dinner?

So, what do insects eat? That depends on the insect, of course. Many insects feast on plants. Caterpillars and grasshoppers have developed very strong jaws to chew on the leaves they eat. Most termites prefer to eat the woody parts of plants, while some beetle grubs prefer to eat rotting wood and seeds. South American heliconiid butterflies like to drink urine!

Insects may also make meals of other insects or small animals like spiders, snails, and tadpoles. Some hunters, like the tiger beetle, may run after their prey. Others, like the praying mantis, sit quietly waiting for lunch to walk close enough to grab. Still others trap their prey. The ant lion larva forms a funnel-shaped trap as it buries itself in sand and waits for an ant. It tosses up sand to make the ant topple down the funnel and into its jaws. Some insects, like mosquitoes, prefer to drink blood.

Super Sippers

Most moths and butterflies have a special mouthpart called a **proboscis**. Shaped like a drinking straw, the proboscis lets these insects sip on the nectar deep inside flowers. Some moths have no mouthparts at all. They live only long enough to breed.

Did You Know?

Praying mantises are fierce and fast **predators.** They usually eat insects, but have been known to catch and eat small lizards or even hummingbirds!

Water scorpions hang upside down beneath the water's surface and wait for prey to swim close. They quickly reach out and grab insect larvae, worms, or even tadpoles with their front legs, then suck out the bodily fluids with a tubelike mouthpart.

Home Is Where the Larva Is

Where is home when you are an insect? Well, it could be under the ground, in a plant stem, or underwater. For some insects, a simple hole or burrow will do. Several larvae, like bagworms and caddis-flies, use silk to wrap themselves in leaves, tiny pebbles, or sticks to make portable, protective apartments.

Many insects go a step further and build complex homes using saliva, mud, wax, or even poop! Ants mix soil with their own spit to make cement that they use when tunneling underground. Honey bees have glands in their abdomens that make wax. They use the wax to build combs where they keep honey and young bees. Some wasps live in paper houses. They chew wood into a paste and then use their jaws to form little compartments (or **cells**). A coating of saliva makes the nest waterproof.

Ant Plant

The hollow thorns of an acacia tree make a perfect home for one **species** of ant. The ants help the plant by chasing off anything that might harm it—from beetles to cows. They will even prune nearby plants to make sure the acacia gets enough sun.

Did You Know?

Some Chinese legends say that Ts'ai Lun got the idea to invent paper from watching wasps as they chewed wood and mixed it with their own saliva to make paper nests.

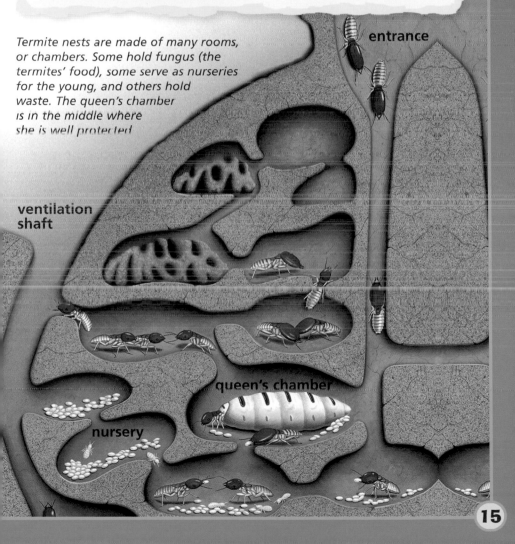

Termite nests are made of many rooms, or chambers. Some hold fungus (the termites' food), some serve as nurseries for the young, and others hold waste. The queen's chamber is in the middle where she is well protected.

entrance

ventilation shaft

queen's chamber

nursery

15

Many Legs Make Light Work

Some insect homes can be pretty amazing, but even more incredible are the insect communities inside. Most wasps and bees and all ants and termites live in groups called colonies. Each **colony** is made up of members that each have a certain job to do. By working together, they are able to protect the nest, provide food for everyone, and raise young.

Ant colonies are good examples of insect communities. Every colony has one queen. Her only job is to lay eggs. There are a few males that mate with the queen and leave soon after. All the rest of the ants are females. Large ants, called soldiers, guard the nest. Worker ants have many jobs. They build the nest, look for food, take care of the young, or clean up waste from the colony.

Blind Ambition

Most worker termites are blind, yet they are able to build very large, complicated nests like this one. These nests can be 10 feet high and are home to millions of termites!

Did You Know?

A honey bee hive must stay at around 93 degrees to hatch and raise the larvae. When the hive gets too hot, the worker bees will fan their wings to cool it off. If it gets too cold, they huddle together in the nursery to heat it up.

Leaf cutter ants are among the only creatures on earth (besides humans) that farm their own food. Millions of ants work together to maintain "gardens" of leaves that grow the fungus they eat.

Staying Alive

It's a dangerous world out there for insects. When you are as small as they are, it's easy to become prey for birds, lizards, or even other insects! But insects aren't completely helpless— they have all kinds of ways to stay alive.

One of the best ways to keep predators away is to be unpleasant. Wasps and bees have painful stings to tell the world, "Stay away!" Some insects are poisonous and "wear" bright red, yellow, or orange. When predators see these colors, they know they need to find something else to eat. Certain beetles are able to squirt burning hot chemicals that blind or poison their attackers. Some sneaky insects even pretend to be dangerous by looking like insects that really are.

In the end, the best way to stay alive is to stay out of sight—by hiding underground, blending in with surroundings, or (like moths) going out only at night.

Bloody Business

This beetle can't fly, but when attacked, it can spit out a drop of its own blood! If the sight of blood isn't enough, the taste usually is. The blood has chemicals in it that will make an attacker very sick.

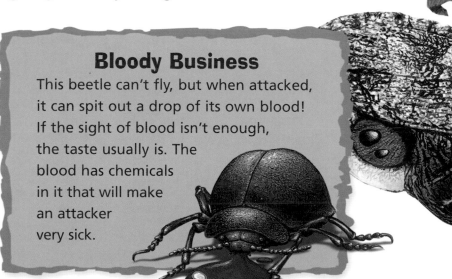

18

Don't Touch!

What's small, soft, furry, and stings when you touch it? This puss moth caterpillar looks like a harmless ball of fluff. But if touched, spines hidden beneath the hairs release a strong venom that causes a painful rash—and sends attackers running.

Usually, these peanut bugs go unnoticed, but when spotted by a hungry bird, they snap their wings open. The two dark wing spots look just like big eyes and usually scare the predator away.

Masters of Disguise

There are insects everywhere, and chances are, you aren't seeing ALL of them. This is because many insects use **camouflage** to stay hidden. Insects have developed ways to look like twigs, dead leaves, flowers, or even small piles of pebbles.

Most insects spend a lot of time on and around plants. It's not surprising that many insects look like plant parts. Some treehoppers have bodies that look like thorns, while the colorful orchid mantis has a body that resembles a delicate pink or white flower. Stick insects are just what they sound like—insects that look exactly like sticks. You probably wouldn't notice a stick insect's eggs either—they are camouflaged to look like seeds.

Some larvae use camouflage to protect their soft bodies. Caddis-fly larvae use silk to cover themselves with tiny pebbles or sand to blend in with their lake-bottom environment. Many cocoons look like dead leaves to hide the pupa inside.

Dead or Alive?

When you think of butterflies, you probably imagine bright colors and pretty patterns. You probably wouldn't notice this resting Indian leaf butterfly. With wings closed, it looks like a dead leaf. But when open, it is painted in shades of bright orange and blue.

Tricky Stick

Can you spot the insect in this picture? Twig insects are experts at hiding—right out in the open. They can be as small as an ant or almost as long as your arm. Some can even change colors to match their surroundings!

When this leaf insect from Malaysia stays completely still or sways in the breeze among the leaves, it would be very difficult to spot—even for a hungry bird.

Glossary

arthropod: An animal with jointed legs and an exoskeleton. This group of animals includes insects, spiders, crabs, scorpions, centipedes, millipedes, ticks, and mites.

camouflage: Colors, body shapes, or patterns that make an animal blend in with its surroundings.

cell: A small compartment. Honey bees and some wasps make nests that are made up of many individual cells. Most cells are used to store food or a single egg. "Cell" comes from the Latin word *cella,* which means "storeroom" or "chamber."

cocoon: A covering of silk, mud, wood, or leaves. It protects the developing pupa inside. Cocoon comes from *coco,* a French word for "shell."

colony: A group of animals of the same species that live and work together.

exoskeleton: This word comes from the Greek words *exo,* which means "outside," and *skeletos,* which means "dried up" or "hard." An insect's exoskeleton is made of many pieces that are joined with a softer material that helps it bend.

metamorphosis: The sometimes drastic change of shape that all insects go through to grow. Two Greek words—*meta,* meaning "change," and *morphe,* meaning "form" or "shape"—make up this word.

palp: A sense organ near the mouth that an insect uses to taste its food. This word comes from the Latin word *palpare,* which means "to feel."

predator: An animal or insect that hunts other animals to eat.

proboscis: A mouthpart shaped like a straw that is found on butterflies, honey bees, mosquitoes, and some other insects. It is used to suck up liquid food (like nectar or blood).

pupa: A stage that an insect goes through to finish complete metamorphosis. While a pupa, the insect's body parts break down and adult features form. *Pupa* is the Latin word for "doll."

species: A group of living things (plants or animals) that have enough in common to be able to reproduce.

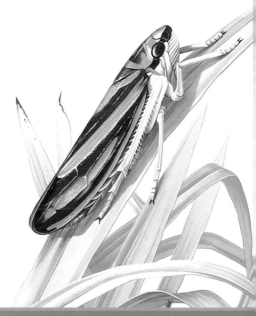